WHY WE L🐾VE DOGS

A Bark & Smile Book
KIM LEVIN

Andrews McMeel
Publishing

Kansas City

www.andrewsmcmeel.com

00 01 02 TWP 10 9 8 7 6

ISBN: 0-8362-6971-3

Library of Congress Catalog Card Number: 98-85159

www/barkandsmile.com

**This book is dedicated to my parents,
and all the dogs I've loved in my life:**

**Susie Q
Sparky
Taffy
Champ
Kelly
Magee
Molly Malone
Katie**

Acknowledgments

Why We Love Dogs is a lifetime of work all rolled up in a book. While the photographs are a compilation of my best work these past few years, my love of dogs started at birth. I grew up in a home that was never without a dog. Dogs have always been a significant part of my life.

When I set out to create a book of my dog portraits, I wanted it to be more than a picture book. I wanted it to express all the reasons why people have dogs in the first place. Simply put, I wanted it to make people laugh and cry at the same time. I hope you will.

Now for my gratitude to those who have helped make *Why We Love Dogs* a reality. Thank you to Jim Andrews at Andrews McMeel Publishing, who was the first person to see the possibilities in my photographs. To Jake Morrissey, my editor, for giving me the opportunity of a lifetime: producing a book of my dog portraits. I want to thank him and Nora Donaghy for their patience and guidance through the editing and production process. I also want to express my gratitude to Steve Gabe, my lawyer, whose endless efforts and passion for "making this happen" are much appreciated.

To my parents, who taught me how the love of a dog can enrich your life, I want to say thank you for all your support and love. We always knew that our love of dogs would lead somewhere; we just didn't know where. To Ricky, you're not just a great brother but a best friend, and I thank you for all the time you have spent giving me advice and guidance regarding my pet portrait business. To my grandmother, who had the insight to see my "kindness to animals" was different than any of her other grandchildren. I am happy you are here to see my tribute to them.

To Johnny, I am so happy we have found each other after all these years. I thank you for your constant support and love.

To all the owners of the dogs I have photographed, thank you for your interest in my photography and your trust with your pets. I truly enjoyed taking your dog's portraits.

To all the dogs I have loved. You are all very special to me. A few sentences about the ones who made a difference in my life. Suzy Q, the dachshund. You lasted fifteen years even with a bad back. Taffy, the beagle. You were my playmate when I was young. The Great Kelly, our first Irish setter. If only you had lived longer. Magee, our second Irish setter. You were regal and stubborn but we loved you anyway. Mollie Malone, our third setter and family favorite. Your smile and heart were larger than most humans'. And last, Katie, the mutt. You are the smartest, wittiest dog we've ever had. We have said you should be in pictures. And now you are.

Last, to all the people who have never experienced the richness a dog can add to your life: Maybe this book will make the difference.

—K.L.

WHY WE L🐾VE DOGS

because they are loyal

because they're inquisitive

because they're so cute

because they're stubborn

because they carry our groceries

because they look alike

because they are
down on their luck

because sometimes they're sad

because they get confused easily

because they stand
out in a crowd

because they have attitude

because they smirk

because they're handsome

**because they have
puppy-dog eyes**

because they howl

because they like their tummies rubbed

because they tease

because they like to lounge

because they relax

because they enjoy the moment

because they look us in the eye

because they're limber

because they get the blues

because they like cats

because they're scruffy

because they're curious

because they stare

because they are indignant

because they make themselves
right at home

because they're sly

because they follow the leader

because they listen
(sometimes)

because they never let us down

because they have funny faces

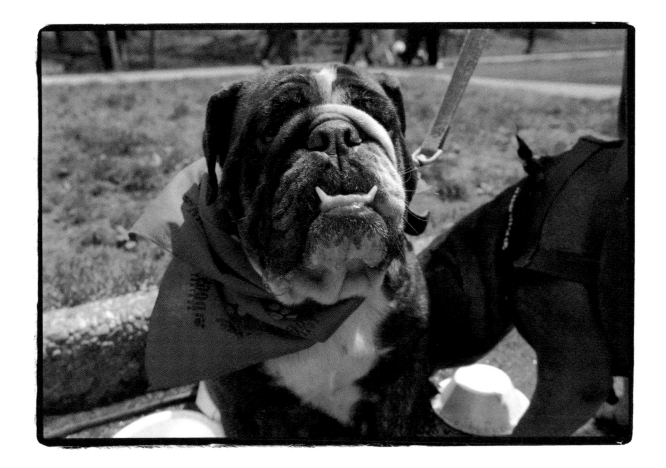

**because they pay
attention to us**

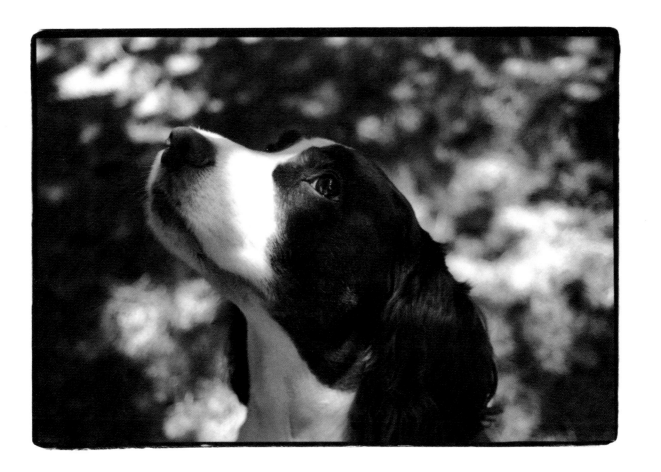

because they love to nuzzle

because they sit funny

because they wonder

because they never complain

because they're shy

because they swim

**because they look bigger
than they really are**

because they lick

because they are subtle

**because they have eyes
only for us**

because they stretch

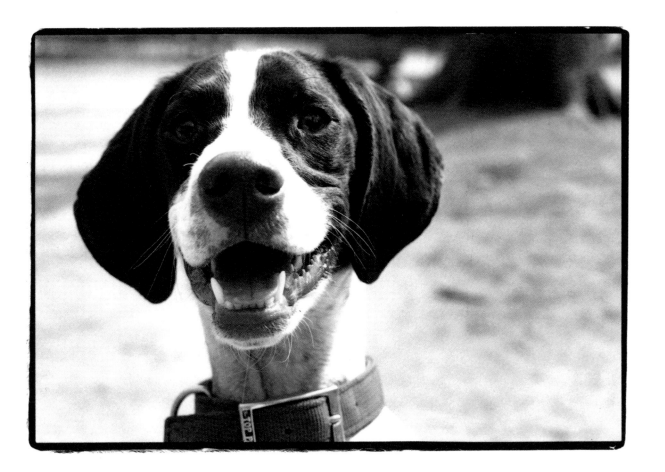